I0150804

The Big Sneeze

The Big Sneeze

Story by
Julia Lane Widdop

Illustrated by
Jeanette Falconetti

Dreamtime Press * Grand Junction, Colorado

Published by Dreamtime Press
3290 Valley View Drive
Grand Junction, CO 81503
1-888-262-5642

Text Copyright 2010 by Julia Lane Widdop
Illustrations Copyright 2010 by Jeanette Falconetti

All rights reserved.

No part of this book may be reproduced or transmitted in any form or by any means,
electronic or mechanical, including photocopying, recording or by any information storage
or retrieval system, without permission in writing from the copyright holders.

The Big Sneeze - Story by Julia Lane Widdop - Illustrated by Jeanette Falconetti

ISBN: 9780982399910
LCCN: 2010926155

Juvenile Creative Nonfiction/ Science & Nature/ Environmental Science & Ecosystems

The Big Sneeze
First Edition
Available at
www.DreamtimePress.com
www.DreamtimeGalleries.com

Book Travel Log tracking the travels of this book at:
www.DreamtimePress.com

Dedication

With Aloha to:

Kenneth, my grandson who inspired this book;
Michael, who supported me in so many ways;
Terry, who helped me with design and production; and
Jeanette, who brought the story to life with her wonderful watercolors.

Also from Jeanette to:

Jerry, for his patience and loving support of my watercolor addiction;
My studio and workshop artist friends, for their helpful critiques and inspiration; and
Julia, for allowing me to illustrate her vision of "The Big Sneeze."

One day The Universe sneezed.
It was a very loud sneeze.
Scientists call it the Big Bang,
but it was really a Big Sneeze.

Bits of energy flew out all over the place.

Jeanette Falconetti

Some pieces became stars.
As energy spread through the universe
it cooled and slowed down.
Some bigger bits became moons and planets.
As the planets cooled some were covered with water.

Jeanette Falconett

Fast vi-brat-ing bits of energy
were floating in that water.
Scientists call the swamp
the pri-mor-di-al (first) soup.

Jeanette Falconetti

Water was e-vap-o-rating and raining
into the swamp and then evaporating again.
This caused big storms.
Energy from the water flew around
in the form of lightning.
Lightning struck the primordial soup
making the energy bits band together.
They became tiny gooey bits
that could absorb energy from the soup.
Yum!

Jeanette Falconetti

The gooey bits realized
they could suck energy
from the mud below
and the sunshine above.

So they spread roots
out into the mud
and formed
thin layers of flat roots
above the water.

We call those leaves.
Thus plants were formed.

Hooray!

Jeanette Falconetti

Some gooey bits learned
how to grow tails
and other wonderful things
so that they could move around.
Thus, animals were formed.
Whoopee!

Jeanette Falconetti

Animals learned to get energy by eating plants.

Jeanette Falconetti

When animals died,
they settled into the mud
and were absorbed by the plant roots.

Thus the energy was recycled.

Yeah!

Gradually water evaporated
uncovering rocks and dirt.

Rock is the form energy takes
when it is so cool and dense
it doesn't move at all.

But plants found
that as long as there was some water
they could suck energy
from the dirt and rocks.

Jeanette Falconetti

Some sea animals crawled onto the land
to eat plants living there, getting energy
from the dirt and sun.

This is how energy was passed
on to the animals.

Thus energy changes form.

Jeanette Falconetti

When plants didn't have water
they couldn't suck energy so
they settled back down
and returned their energy to the dirt.

Thus energy was recycled.

Jeanette Falconetti

When animals die
they return their energy to the dirt
where plants can get it again.

Round and round it goes.

This is the story of recycling energy or

The Big Sneeze.

(Cover your mouth)

Jeanette Falconetti

Tracking The Big Sneeze Around the World

We are always happy when one of our books finds a permanent and happy home in your library, but we also love to hear about the travels of our books from reader to reader, so we hope you will make an entry in our book travel log and tell us where you read The Big Sneeze, and how you liked it. Just go to www.DreamtimePress.com and click on the Book Travel Log tab and tell us where in the world The Big Sneeze is now.

www.ingramcontent.com/pod-product-compliance
Lightning Source LLC
LaVergne TN
LVHW072110070426
835509LV00002B/95